Potty Training Is Easier Than You Think:

Everything You Need To Know About Potty Training

Jennifer N. Smith

CONTENTS

Everything You Need To Know About Potty Training

Chapter 1- Preparing for Potty Training

Before you begin potty training, you are going to have to take a few steps to not only prepare your child for the process but yourself as well. The first thing that you have to do when you are preparing for potty training is to ensure that **your child is ready to potty train.**

Beginning potty training when your child is not ready could cause training to take longer and your child to develop anxiety toward potty training.

Signs Your Child is Ready To Potty Train

1. Taking their own diaper off when it is soiled.
2. Hiding when they dirty their diaper.
3. Showing interest in others that are using the restroom.
4. Being able to sleep through a nap and awake with a dry diaper.
5. Telling you that they have soiled their diaper or that they need to go.

If your child is showing two or more of these signs, then chances are, they are ready to begin potty training.

Once the child is showing signs that he or she is ready to

start potty training, it is time to prepare yourself. It can seem completely overwhelming to teach a child which has become accustom to using a diaper not to use a diaper. Potty training can be frustrating and it can be a messy experience if you are not prepared for what lies ahead**. It is also important for you to understand that one of the main reasons that potty training fails, besides the child not being ready to potty train is because the parent is not prepared.**

If you are not ready 100 percent mentally to begin potty training your child, you need to wait until you are because once you begin, it is a very bad idea to stop and go back to diapers. Stopping and starting potty training will only confuse the child and that is that last thing that you want to happen while you are trying to get them to use the toilet.

Do not compare your child to other children when it comes to potty training. Each child will be prepared to potty train when they are prepared to potty train and not a moment earlier.

Of course, life is going to happen and there are going to be times when you are going to have to use a diaper or a pull up type diaper. This should only happen when you do not know if you will have access to a bathroom. When you begin potty training, you need to ensure that you are not going to be using diapers at any point. This may mean that you have to take a few days off of work or not leave the house while you are potty training.

Which of course means that the second step to preparing yourself for potty training is ensuring that you will have the time to potty train and that you will not be interrupted. Jumping up one morning and deciding that you are going to begin potty training is never going to work because chances are, you are going to need to run to the store or go visit someone or leave the house for one of a million reasons. When you are potty training your child, if you want it to be a smooth process and you want it to be done quickly, you will have to set some time aside in order to work through the entire process.

Next, you will have to make a few purchases. You can either purchase a potty seat that goes over the regular toilet seat or you can purchase a small potty for your child. What you purchase will depend on what technique you choose to use and what your personal preferences are. Personally, I suggest that you purchase a small potty for your child as it can be moved from room to room and your child will always have access to it, even when someone else is in the bathroom. One thing that you should remember when you are purchasing a small potty or a potty seat is access.

When you purchase a **small potty** , the child does not have to have your help getting onto it nor do they have to climb in order to get onto it. A small potty will also allow them to keep their feet flat on the floor which will make a bowel movement much easier.

If you purchase a **potty seat**, you will have to decide if you will be lifting the child onto the potty each time they have to go, or if you will purchase a step or stool for them to climb up on. If you do purchase a step or stool, you should make sure that the child is able to place their feet flat on the stool as they are sitting on the toilet. <u>**I do not suggest that you lift the child and allow their legs to dangle as this position pinches the bowels shut and makes it much harder for the child to relieve himself or herself.**</u>

Purchasing the potty seat in advance is a great idea because it will allow the child to get used to it and it will allow the transition from diaper to potty to be smoother. If you plan on ever leaving your house, you will also want to purchase a travel potty seat. The openings in most public toilets are much larger than the openings in our toilets at home, which means it will be much easier for your child to fall in. ***All it takes is one time and your child will not want to use any toilet for a very long time.***

New underwear is another item that you will need to purchase. **I would suggest purchasing underwear with your child's favorite character on them because it will motivate them to use the toilet.** Simply telling them not to potty on their favorite character is often motivation enough for them to let you know when they need to go.

Some people suggest training pants like pull-up style diaper, while these are fine to use on occasion such as when you will be going to the grocery store, I do not suggest that you use them all of the time. The reason for this is because they feel much like a diaper however when you purchase them underwear, you will be able to emphasize what a **big boy or a big girl** they are. They will recognize that their underwear is the same as their father's or mother's.

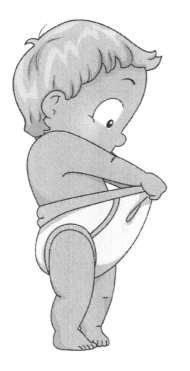

Beginning potty training when your child is not ready could cause training to take longer and your child to develop anxiety toward potty training.

You may also choose to purchase a few small rewards. Some people suggest offering a few pieces of candy when the child uses the potty, however other's do not feel that this is a healthy option and instead choose to create a rewards chart, giving the child stars each time they use the potty successfully.

A timer will come in handy as well and it needs to be one that makes sound that is loud enough for your child to hear. The timer will be used as a reminder for your child to use the bathroom because as we all know; a child can become distracted and completely forget to go to the bathroom until it is too late. We also know that it is very easy for us to become distracted when we are trying to potty train a child because after all, we are not the one that needs to go to the bathroom. The timer is going to be a reminder for both you and your child, to ensure that the child is on the potty on a regular basis.

It is also important for you to understand that one of the main reasons that potty training fails, besides the child not being ready to potty train is because the parent is not prepared.

Do not compare your child to other children when it comes to potty training. Each child will be prepared to potty train when they are prepared to potty train and not a moment earlier. Take for example my children. My oldest son was potty trained the day after his second birthday. He had one accident and then never had another. My daughter basically potty trained herself at the age of one because she had access to a little potty at all times while my youngest son did not potty train until he was a bit over three years old and the process was not an easy one.

You should also not compare yourself to other mothers who have potty trained or are potty training their children. If you take my children as an example, you can see that no amount of experience is going to ensure you are able to potty train a child quickly. You should not allow yourself to feel like a failure when it comes to potty training no matter how long it takes or how hard it may seem at the time.

Finally, after you have prepared yourself for potty training your child, you will need to prepare your child for potty training. **<u>The first thing that you want to do is to create the right mindset for your child when it comes to potty training.</u>** You can do this by focusing on the positives of potty training. Talk about the new underwear that your child will be wearing, how they will be using the potty like mommy and daddy, how they will be a big boy or girl when they start using the potty.

One thing that you do not want to do is make them feel like a baby for wearing diapers or that wearing a diaper is gross. In other words, do not focus on the **negatives** of wearing a diaper, but instead on the **positives** of using the potty.

The next step is to use potty talk. Many parents use pee pee or poopoo when they talk about their child eliminating however, many professionals suggest that you should use words such as urinate or defecate so that the child is not embarrassed later in life by this baby talk.

It is also important that you let your child know that going to the bathroom is natural and that it is not something that is gross or smelly or nasty. Letting them know that it is completely natural is going to help them feel more comfortable when you are potty training them.

The first thing that you want to do is to create the right mindset for your child when it comes to potty training. You can do this by focusing on the positives of potty training.

<u>**Praise grown up behavior,**</u> not just when the child uses the potty, but when they do not spill their cup, when they are polite or when they share their toys without having to be told to do so. You should not worry about forcing your child to behave too sophisticated when it comes to their behavior, but always praise the big boy or big girl behavior. This will not only help your child feel good about

themselves, but it will reinforce the behavior and make them want to display more big boy or big girl behaviors.

You can also grab a few picture books about potty training and read to your child each night before they go to bed. You don't have to feel like you have to get the child to understand everything about potty training from you reading a book to them, but what you will find is that they become excited about potty training and the process becomes very easy for them.

Besides getting your child in the right mindset, you will also want to go through the motions. **In other words, make sure that you are dressing your child in clothes that would make it easy for them to use the potty in.** For example, make sure that they are wearing pants that are easy to pull down, that do not have a bunch of buttons or clasps to deal with and practice having your child pull them down. You can play little games such as counting to three and seeing if your child can pull his or her pants down in three seconds. This is important to do because when it is time for the child to potty, there is not going to be any time to spare.

Some parents suggest taking the child into the bathroom with them. This allows the parent to not only explain how to sit, wipe and flush, but it allows the child to see it happening. This often gets children very interested in potty training, however, **this is not for everyone**. If you choose to bring the child into the bathroom with you, it is best if you can have the parent of the same sex take the child with them. Of course, some parents are not comfortable with this step and if you are not, then that is perfectly fine simply skip it.

Some professionals also suggest that you purchase a doll that drinks and pottys allowing your child to teach the doll how to use the potty. This can help to make the child feel as if they have some control and understanding over a process that can be quite overwhelming. This is not necessary when it comes to potty training, however some parents feel that it is helpful.

You can also use the actual potty to motivate your child to use it. When my daughter was potty training, we purchased her a small 'throne' with a crown and all types of little jewels all over it. When she would use the potty, it would play music and light up. Of course, this motivated her to use the potty because she wanted to see the light show and hear the music. But you do not have to purchase a potty with all of the bells and whistles if you do not want to. **Even the simplest potty can motivate a child to use it.**

If all of this focus on potty training and potty talk seems to upset your child or bore them, chances are, that they are not ready to go through the process of potty training and you should try again in a few weeks.

Chapter 2- Common Problems Faced During

Potty Training

Before you begin potty training, it is important for you to understand the common problems that are faced during potty training so that you can face them head on and you will know how to handle these problems.

1. Your child has no interest in using the potty

When this happens, you need to make sure that your child is actually ready to start potty training. Most children will begin to show interest in the toilet when they are ready to start potty training if they do not, this is a sign that something more is going on. One thing that may be happening is that your child is feeling a lot of anxiety about using the potty or they may feel that they are under a lot of pressure. You should also make sure that the child is not constipated, and that the child is not afraid of the potty.

Some children are afraid of the sound that a toilet makes when they flush and **they may also be**

Do not become frustrated or upset. Your child is going to learn to use the potty at some point, however, it will be when he or she is ready, not when you think they should be ready.

afraid of falling into the potty. One way to handle this is to never flush the toilet while the child is still on it. Instead, let the child get off of the toilet and flush it themselves. Or flush the toilet when the child has left the room. If the child is afraid of falling in the potty you should make sure that the child has something that they can firmly place their feet on such as a stool. This will make them feel more secure when sitting on the toilet.

2. **Your child has had no problem using the potty, but suddenly is having accidents again**

When you are potty training your child, you have to understand that there are many things that can affect how they use the toilet. Illness, excitement, change in routine, the birth of a sibling or any other event that takes place in the child's life can cause the child to regress a bit. It is important for you to provide reassurance to your child when they are facing a lot of stress or change in their lives and it is very important for you to keep everything in their life as normal as possible. No matter what you do, do not go back to using diapers because this will mean that you have to start the entire process over again. **Stay strong and stick with the training**.

If you notice that your child is not wanting to use the toilet and that they have not been using the toilet as normal, you might want to take your child to the doctor. Diarrhea, constipation, and urinary tract infections can cause a child to not want to use the potty because it is causing them pain. It is important for you to pay attention to the small signs that your child may need to see a doctor, such as not having a bowel movement for several days or having urine that is dark in color and has a strong smell.

3. **Your child refuses to sit on the potty and when asked will say, "NO!"**

This is nothing more than normal defiance that you will face with any child. Your child is trying to be independent and this is your child's way of asserting himself or herself. The child does not want to potty train because it is something that you want them to do, therefore, you need to make potty training seem like it is the child's idea. There are a few different ways for you to handle this type of situation. You can simply make the child believe that it was his or her idea. This is where a potty training doll would come in handy, tell the child that you thought they might want to teach the baby how to use the potty or give them a book about using the potty and tell them that you thought they might need it if they decided they wanted to potty.

When you encounter a problem like this, not only when you are potty training, but anytime, you should remember to keep your cool and to not overreact. Begin by removing anything that your child might feel is pressuring them to do what you want them to do and reassure yourself and the child that they can make the decision on their own. **Do not become frustrated or upset.** Your child is going to learn to use the potty at some point, however, it will be when he or she is ready, not when you think they should be ready.

4. **Your child knows when he or she needs to have a bowel movement but is still wetting their pants.**

This is a common issue and it is nothing to be concerned about. Children become more aware of when they need to have a bowel movement before they understand that they need to urinate. They also gain more control over their bowels before there are able to control their bladder. With time and practice as well as patience, they will stop wetting themselves and will soon be using the potty all of the time.

5. **Your son insists on sitting down when he is urinating.**

Some people become upset when their son wants to sit down while he is urinating, but this is perfectly normal and is not something that you should become upset about. The child will stand when he is ready and having him sit on the potty is a lot less messy than teaching him how to stand when potty training. Wait until he is fully potty trained and his hips are above the seat of the toilet before you worry about teaching him how to stand when he urinates.

6. **Your child wants to play with feces.**

There is something very interesting about feces to the mind of a child and while not everyone talks about this, everyone experiences it at one point or another. This can be a bit tricky to deal with because as stated earlier in this book, we do not want to make the child feel as if having a bowel movement or urinating is something that is gross or unnatural however we do want to make sure that they are not playing with feces. The way to handle this is to sternly explain that this is not something we touch but do not yell at your child and upset him or her.

7. **Your child has accidents while you are potty training.**

Accidents are going to happen and there is no reason for you or your child to become upset by them. Accidents do not mean that you are failing at potty training your child or that they are failing at learning how to use the potty it simply means they had an accident. Do not make a big deal out of it, instead, make light of it and move on. Laugh, tell your child that they peed on their favorite character and have them help you put the underwear in the washer. Don't dwell on the accident.

8. **Your child tells you that they need a diaper when they need to have a bowel movement or they will only go in one specific place.**

This is a sign that your child is not emotionally ready to potty train while they may be physically ready. This is where a small potty could come in handy. If you have a small potty, you can place it in the area that the child wants to have the bowel movement. This will get the child use to using the potty while allowing the child to feel comfortable in the special place. If the child wants to use a diaper, you can allow the child to

use the diaper, but suggest that they use it in the
bathroom.

9. **Your child wets the bed.**

Chances are, your child is going to wet the bed. Using
night time pants is perfectly fine when you are first
beginning to potty train. Have the child use the potty
before they go to bed, remind the child that if he or
she wakes up in the middle of the night and needs to
go to the bathroom all they need to do is to call out for
you and make sure that the child uses the potty first
thing in the morning. This will cut down on a lot of
accidents and soon you will find that the overnight
pants are dry in the mornings.

10. **Your child will only go to the bathroom with
one person.**

This is perfectly normal. You are the one that is potty
training the child and the child is comfortable with
having you in the bathroom with them. The problem
comes when the parent does not slowly withdraw
themselves from the bathroom while the child is using
it. Once the child grasps the idea of using the toilet
and is able to clean themselves well, you are no longer
needed in the bathroom and need to allow your child
to be independent.

These are the most common problems that you are going to face while you are potty training your child. Of course, there are other problems that are going to come up along the way, **but the key to getting through these problems is to keep your cool and to praise your child when they are successful at using the potty.**

There is no reason to make your child feel poorly about accidents and there is no reason for you to feel poorly about yourself when your child has an accident. Instead, focus on the positives and keep going.

Chapter 3- Understanding What Does Not Work

Parents have been potty training their children for a very long time and one thing that they have learned is what does not work.

The first thing that you need to know when it comes to understanding what does not work when it comes to potty training is that you cannot start too soon. Many people hear stories of children who were potty trained at a very early age and they want their children to potty train early as well. They look at potty training early on as proof of their success at parenting, however, that is not the case.

The final mistake that I want to address is parents worrying too much about potty training. Chances are that your child is not going to be going to high school wearing a diaper, they will learn how to use the potty eventually and while cleaning up messes may be frustrating and time consuming, it will be over soon and believe it or not, you are going to miss changing those little diapers one day.

I stated earlier in the book that my daughter potty trained at a very early age, however, my youngest son took longer than both of his siblings. This had nothing to do with my parenting skills and I understood that it was not a competition. You have to remember this as well. **If you start your child too early, it is only going to prolong the process because their bodies simply are not ready to start potty training.**

If you do want to start early, I suggest that you purchase a small potty to keep in the main room of your house. Allow your child to use it when he or she wants, letting them take control of their own potty training, but do not try and force them to potty train early.

Many parents also believe that if they show their child that they are disappointed in them for having an accident, the child will try harder next time. This simply is not true. You have to remember that this is a completely new experience for your child and they are trying as hard as they can, however, they are used to using a diaper and can forget that they are supposed to use the potty. **Instead of showing disappointment, you should encourage your child, letting the child know that you are not angry with them for having the accident.** You should also let the child know that you believe in them and that they can use the potty next time instead of having an accident.

I spoke earlier about giving rewards, but one mistake that many parents make is setting the bar too high and giving rewards that are far too large. Rewarding your child with a sticker or a few M&M's is one thing, but telling your child that you will take him or her to the zoo if they stop wearing a diaper is only going to cause anger and frustration. If the child's body is not ready to potty train, the child is going to feel as if they are fighting against their own body and that can lead to them feeling like a failure. Losing a reward that is large can also be upsetting for the child as well, especially when the child knows that he or she has tried their best.

<u>Don't ever try to force your child to go to the bathroom or make them sit on the toilet as some form of punishment because they did not go</u>. Your child knows his or her own body, if they tell you that they do not have to go, accept that they know and let them go back to their day. If, however, you find that the child is having an accident right after getting off of the potty or holding it until they are able to sneak away to a corner, you have to make a

21

choice. The first choice would be to accept, that your child is not emotionally ready to begin potty training and wait a few weeks before trying again. The second option is to help your child relax while they are on the potty. This can be done by simply reading them a book. This will also keep the child on the potty longer without a fuss and hopefully it will get the child to use the potty.

One huge mistake that many parents make is to begin potty training during a time of stress for either the entire family, for the parents or for the child. You should never try to begin potty training when you or the child are under an unusual amount of stress. Many parents try to potty train their children in an attempt to save money. The family is depending on the money that is spent on diapers, however, the child simply is not ready to begin potty training. This leads to hurt feelings as well as upset parents and children on top of the stress that they are already dealing with. Instead, find a different way to save money, for example, try using coupons or rewards at your favorite store to purchase the diapers or simply purchase a cheaper brand. Remember, just because your pocketbook says that it is time to potty train does not mean that your child's body will agree.

Never set a deadline for your child when it comes to potty training. **Your child is going to have to deal with enough deadlines in his or her life, potty training should not be one of them.** Your child's body is going to be the one that determines when the child is completely potty trained. Even after the child is potty trained, you need to understand that the child is going to have accidents on occasion. This does not mean that they are not fully potty trained.

It is also important for you to understand that if you do set a deadline, you are doing nothing more than setting yourself as well as your child up for failure. **You have to take your lifestyle into consideration.** Children who attend daycare are going to take longer to potty train because they are not getting the same one on one attention that a child who stays home with a parent would get. If you have shared custody of your child it could take longer to potty train him or her, depending on what is going on at the other parent's home. If the child is a special needs child, you will start later and it is going to take more patience than it would to potty train another child.

Trust your instincts when it comes to potty training. Other parents are always going to have an opinion on how you should parent your child and this includes how as well as when you should potty train. You have to remember that you know your child better than anyone and what worked for them may not work for you. Let the parent know that you are thankful for their advice, but you are going to continue to do things the way that you feel is best. Most parents are not going to get offended because you do not take their advice, they simply enjoy giving their advice.

Another mistake that many parents make when they are potty training their child is that they blow off the child's

fears. You have to remember that a child has no idea how a toilet works, all they know is if you flush, it goes down. In their minds, that means that they can go down as well. Some children may also be afraid of what will come up while they are sitting on the potty. Neither of these fears should be ignored. **These fears are as real to your child as any fear that you might have and they need to know that**

they will be okay. Being afraid of the loud flushing sound is another common fear that should be addressed and not ignored.

The final mistake that I want to address is parents worrying too much about potty training. Chances are that your child is not going to be going to high school wearing a diaper, they will learn how to use the potty eventually and while cleaning up messes may be frustrating and time consuming, it will be over soon and believe it or not, you are going to miss changing those little diapers one day. **There really is no reason to stress, worry or get upset about potty training.** Instead, let it happen naturally without a ton of pressure from you or other adults such as grandparents.

Knowing the common mistakes that most people make while they are potty training their child is a great way to make sure you do not make the same mistakes. If you find yourself starting to make one of these mistakes, simply acknowledge what you are doing and move on to something else.

Most importantly, you should never withhold love from your child when they are trying to potty train. In fact, you should never withhold love from your child at all. This is not a form of discipline and it will teach your child that if they are unable to do what you say, you will no longer love them and no one wants to make their child feel that way.

Chapter 4- Potty Training Tips For Boys

Raising a boy is completely different than raising a girl and so is potty training a boy. In this chapter, I want to focus on the boys for a little bit. We will focus on the girls in the next chapter, but I want to give you some tips that will help you when it comes to potty training a boy.

It is suggested that you can begin potty training a boy as early as 18 months old, but some boys may not be ready for potty training until after their third birthday. Many professionals also believe that it takes a little bit longer for boys to be potty trained than it does for girls because boys are more likely to ignore what their bodies are saying and continue on with playing or whatever activity they are involved in. **It is best to wait until your son is between the ages of two and three before you start potty training.**

S i m p l y   g e t t i n g   h i m   u s e d   t o
s i t t i n g   o n   t h e   t o i l e t   i s   g o i n g
t o   m a k e   p o t t y   t r a i n i n g   r u n
m u c h   s m o o t h e r .

Instead of jumping into potty training, let the child sit on the potty for a little while before you begin training. **Simply getting him used to sitting on the toilet is going to make potty training run much smoother.** You want to start him out sitting because at the age where a child is ready to potty train, they do not have the ability to stand in front of a toilet and urinate nor will they have any ability to aim.

You will want to make sure that you purchase a potty seat or a small potty that has a small cup on the front of it to ensure that he does not urinate all over the room. Sitting is the easiest way to potty train a child because they simply are not tall enough to stand in front of a toilet and urinate. It is also important for you to allow the child to sit while potty training until the child has learned how to control his bowels, simply because you do not want him to end up having a bowel movement on the floor while trying to stand and use the potty. **Save the standing for later, when the child has learned how to control his bowels and will be better at learning how to aim.**

Some people suggest potty training your son to urinate on a tree outside. While this might be an easy way to potty train a child, the reality is that you are not really potty training them as much as you are teaching the child to go outside and urinate on a tree. This can backfire and I have seen it happen in the past. Teaching her child to urinate on a tree would be easier because the child found this activity fun. It was no longer fun when the child would wake up in the middle of the night and need to be taken outside to urinate on the tree because he did not associate the toilet with urinating. **We have to be very careful what we are teaching our children.**

Make sure that when you are beginning to potty train that you dress your child in clothing that is very easy for him to remove**. Some parents think that it is better to allow the child to run around the house naked for a few days until they are used to using the potty and if that method works well for you then that is great.**

You will, however, have to explain to unexpected company why your child is naked and depending on who shows up, that could be quite embarrassing. Simply letting the child **run around in a tee shirt and his new underwear** will ensure that he is able to pull his underwear down in time to get onto the toilet and relieve himself.

Just like when you are potty training a girl, you will want to use a rewards system with your son as well. Stickers are a great reward and if your child knows anything about the military, placing them on his shirt like badges and letting him show them off to other family members is going to be a great motivator.

Praise your child when they use the potty. This is going to be the same for a boy or for a girl. Do not just simply say good job, here is your sticker and walk away. **Get excited.** When your son sees you getting excited about something he has accomplished, he is going to get excited as well and that is what is going to motivate him to continue the behavior.

Common Problems Boys Face When Potty Training

Boys are going to face their own set of problems when they are potty training, but the issues are very easily remedied if you know ahead of time what you are looking for.

1. You have no problem potty training your son to have a bowel movement in the toilet but find him wet regularly. This is a common problem with many boys and the reason for this is because they have simply forgotten to go to the bathroom. They are completely caught up in what they are doing and are not paying attention to anything else.

    It may also be because you are able to tell when the child is going to have a bowel movement and you take action to get them into the bathroom. However, you cannot tell when a child is urinating, short of finding the puddle below them, because they do not make a face or grunt as they would if they were having a bowel movement.

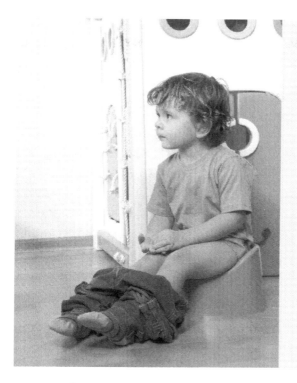

It is also important for you to allow the child to sit while potty training until the child has learned how to control his bowels, simply because you do not want him to end up having a bowel movement on the floor while trying to stand and use the potty. Save the standing for later, when the child has learned how to control his bowels and will be better at learning how to aim.

The way to remedy this is simple. **Set a timer for 20 minutes, letting your son know that when the timer goes off, you will be taking him to use the toilet and follow through with what you have said, no matter what you are doing**.

2. You find that your son is urinating in places other than the potty. This is one of those things that happens that most people do not want to talk about and they do now want to ask their friend's advice about and that is why I feel it is important to cover the topic. If this is happening mostly at night, you need to understand why. **Perhaps your son is not able to make it to the bathroom when he gets up in**

the middle of the night, if this is the case, putting a small potty in his room for him to use at night would be a good idea.

Of course, he may not be fully awake when he does this in which case it is important for you to ensure he is using the potty before he goes to bed at night and not drinking any liquid within an hour of bed. If this is not the issue, you will need to think about why your child is doing this. Is he resentful because of a recent separation? Did you start working and put him in daycare? Perhaps he is just stressed out about potty training in general. The good news is that whatever the reason, it will pass with time, even if you can't figure out why he is displaying this behavior and I would suggest purchasing several gallons of white vinegar, especially if you have carpet to get the smell out.

3. Your son is having bowel movements in his pants, long after being potty trained. This is not a common problem, but it is one that many doctors see and it is one that means our child needs to see a doctor. Most often, this is caused from being potty trained too early, however, when it continues on after the child is of school age, the doctors need to address it because it could be a variety of different issues. You should never assume that your child is displaying this behavior because he is choosing to or because he wants attention. This is very embarrassing for your child and should be handled with care.

4. There are times when the child will want to remain the baby, not wanting to potty train or act his age.

When this happens, it is best to expose your child to other children his own age. This is the one time in your child's life where peer pressure will work to his advantage. When your son sees other children his age, especially boys his age not wearing a diaper and not having accidents all day long, he is going to become very motivated to get rid of that diaper and start using the potty like all of his new friends.

Depending on who you ask, you might be told that potty training a boy is very difficult and that it takes a lot longer than it does than potty training a girl. You might be told that boys should only be potty trained by their fathers or that potty training is going to be the hardest thing you have to do.

None of this is true. The only time that these statements are ever true is when you make them true. You have to remember when you are potty training that you are the one in control. While it is important for you to let the child's body decide when it is ready for potty training it is also important for you to remind your child that you are the parent and you know what is best for them, even when it comes to where they eliminate.

Chapter 5- Potty Training Tips For Girls

Maybe you have heard it said that potty training a girl was easier than potty training a boy. Maybe someone who potty trained both boys and girls told you this. You can probably guess that this is, in fact, not the truth. The truth is that girls can begin potty training just a few months earlier than boys can and I believe that is why many people believe that potty training a girl is easier.

Of course, you don't have to worry about teaching a girl about standing up when they urinate or have a discussion about aim which can make potty training a girl seem easier.

One way that you can prepare your daughter for potty training is to allow her to join Mom in the bathroom. She will be able to observe you and will learn from the process. Placing a small potty against one wall in the bathroom will allow her to mock you which will make potty training much easier in the future.

Let her pick out her new panties, show her the cutest ones that you can afford so that she will get excited about wearing them. Tell her that they are just like yours and this will get her even more excited when it comes to potty training.

Another great tip that you can use to make potty training more fun for your daughter is to take her shopping before you begin training. **Let her pick out her new panties, show her the cutest ones that you can afford so that she will get excited about wearing them**. Tell her that they are just like yours and this will get her even more excited when it comes to potty training. It is also important that you let your daughter pick out the potty seat that she wants or make sure you choose something she is going to love.

I spoke earlier in this book about the little musical throne that I purchased my daughter, there was actually a reason that I purchased the throne beside the fact that it lit up and made music. I purchased that particular potty because my daughter was known as the princess and the throne was perfect for her. **Make sure that the potty, you choose for your daughter is perfect for her as well.**

You should never say words like 'gross' or 'nasty', even if she makes a mess because she will not associate the word with the bowel movement, urine or the accident she had, instead, she will associate the word with who she is.

Potty training should be fun for your child. It should not feel like a chore or something that they have to do because mommy and daddy said so. **This means that you need to come up with ways to keep it interesting.** Now we all know how boring it can be to sit on the pot, however, it is what you do afterward with your child that is going to make the difference. Let your child have a few minutes of your time to celebrate her success, get her excited about using the potty and you will find that potty training is no trouble at all.

It is important for you to teach your daughter how to sit as well. If you are using a potty seat on top of your toilet, you need to make sure that she has a stool to place her feet against and that her bottom does not drop below her knees. **This is because when her bottom is lower than her knees when she is using the potty, small amounts of urine will collect in the vagina**. This urine will leak out into her underwear later as she goes about her business and this, of course, could make her think she has had an accident, could cause her to smell or cause many other health issues. You also want to make sure that she is not sitting too far forward on the seat because this can cause accidents or leaks which no one wants to clean up.

The final tip that I have for you in this chapter is to never shame your child when she has an accident. Having an accident is going to be hard enough on her, chances are she will be fighting back the tears and if you shame her, it could cause her to give up altogether. Instead, remind her that she is supposed to use the potty, clean her up and get on with your day.

You will have to teach your daughter to properly wipe

ensuring that no bacteria is introduced into the urinary tract. However, you should not expect a female child under the age of five to be able to wipe herself properly and you should do this for her. Of course, when parents begin potty training, they are always tempted to purchase flushable wipes for their child in hopes that it will make clean up easier, however, this can cause more problems, especially when you are potty training a girl.

These flushable wipes contain chemicals that disrupt the natural, healthy bacteria in and around the vagina. They can also cause irritation and redness which can become painful for the child. Instead of going out and spending money on a product that could make it harder to potty train your child, simply use toilet paper.

After your daughter has used the potty and is all cleaned up, it is time for them to wash their hands. Today, many parents are letting this step slip because they feel that hand sanitizer is going to do the trick, however, there are certain bacteria that not even hand sanitizer will kill. **This is why it is very important for you to teach your child to use soap and water every time they go to the bathroom, lathering for at least 20 seconds before rinsing**.

Because it does take some time to learn how to wipe, it is often not done properly when the child is first learning how to use the potty and this means that you have to keep an eye out for infections. Signs of infection are painful urination, fever, frequent need to urinate, cloudy or even bloody urine, poor appetite and increased accidents.

You may be tempted to go out and purchase a potty doll, or to buy apps that are supposed to help with potty training or any number of other products on the market, however, this is not necessary. You don't have to have all the latest gadgets and gizmos in order to potty train your child. **The truth is, all it really takes is a dedicated parent, a potty and a child that is ready to be potty trained.**

Just like boys face problems when they are potty training, girls do as well. Before we move on to the next chapter I want to talk a little bit about the problems girls can face and what you can do about them.

Common Problems When Potty Training a Girl.

1. Many parents jump into potty training without a plan and use the latest and greatest technique that they saw online, on television or that their friends told them about. This often leads to a lot of disappointment because as I have stated before what works for one child will not work for another. When it comes to potty training your daughter, you know her better than anyone else and it is important for you to choose a plan that will work best for her. **For example, if your daughter is independent, you may want to allow her access to a potty, but not actually make a big deal out of potty training.** On the other hand, if your daughter always needs you to show your approval, making a big deal out of what she is doing is very important to her success.
    Hoping that your child is going to potty train the exact same way your friend's daughter did or even the same way your older daughter did, **is setting her up for failure.**

2. Most mothers understand that they need to make their little girl feel like a big girl when it comes to potty training. When it comes to rewards, little girls will usually want something different than little boys. Of course, stickers are always great, but imagine how hard your daughter would try to use the potty if she knew she could use some lip gloss or chap stick each time that she is successful.

3. Making potty time something that is gross or disgusting is a huge mistake when it comes to potty training a girl. Most little girls do not want to think that what they are doing is gross in any way. They want to feel pretty and even though there is nothing pretty about going to the bathroom, you can take the focus off of what the child is doing and focus on something else, something that she thinks is beautiful. While she sits on the potty, talk to her about flowers or butterflies, unicorns or ponies, anything that will get her mind off of what she is doing. **You should never say words like 'gross' or 'nasty', even if she makes a mess because she will not associate the word with the bowel movement, urine or the accident she had, instead, she will associate the word with who she is.**

4. Rushing is a huge mistake when it comes to potty training your daughter. She should not be rushed onto the toilet, she should not be rushed while on the toilet and she should not be rushed to get off of the toilet. You should also make sure that you never rush your daughter when it comes to potty training in general. You should not make her feel as if she has to be potty trained by a specific date or that it will be her fault that you do not get to go on vacation or shopping if she is not potty trained. It can take from a few days to

several months to potty train depending on the technique that you use how consistent you are and how ready the child is.

Boy or girl, the goal is the same, to get the child out of diapers and to get them to start using the potty on a regular basis. **The final tip that I have for you in this chapter is to never shame your child when she has an accident.** Having an accident is going to be hard enough on her, chances are she will be fighting back the tears and if you shame her, it could cause her to give up altogether. Instead, remind her that she is supposed to use the potty, clean her up and get on with your day.

Chapter 6- Methods For Potty Training

There are many different potty training methods, it seems that almost every parent I talk to has a method of their very own that they are sure will work for everyone. However, the truth is that no method is going to work for everyone because each child is **<u>unique.</u>**

Since there is no single method of potty training that is going to be successful for everyone, in this chapter, I want to go over several methods that you can use. **This will ensure that if one method is not working well for you or your child, you will be able to quickly move on to the next method.**

1. Potty Training At The Weekend

This method is used by many parents that work full time and want to be able to potty train their child in a short amount of time. Some people suggest that you allow the child to remain naked while they are in your home. This is going to be up to you and there are of course ways around this if you are not comfortable with it.

Of course, these are not all of the techniques and you can use a mixture of the techniques or even come up with a technique of your own, as long as it works for you and your child.

Many studies have shown that while it is easier to potty train a child by allowing them to remain naked throughout the process, they have also proven that once the child has clothes on, he or she has no idea what they are supposed to do and quickly regress to messing their pants. However, it is okay for the child to wear training pants while they are sleeping.

You will also need several different little potty seats to sit all around the house. It is recommended that one seat should be in each main area of the house where you and the child will spend your days as well as one in the bathroom.

Another problem with choosing to let your child roam naked around the house is that you will have to plan potty training around the seasons. **You do not want your child running around your house naked if it is cold.**

It is also important that you do not just decide one day that you are going to potty train without first preparing the child. You need to begin talking about potty training about 2-3 weeks before you begin. Purchase a few picture books that will get your child interesting in potty training.

Before you begin, show your child their diapers, that is, what is left of them, and explain that when the diapers run out, there will be no more diapers. Explain to the child that he or she will start using the potty like a big kid.

On the first day, you are going to have to watch for signs that your child needs to potty. As soon as the child begins going, or shows signs of needing to go, you will quickly place the child on the nearest potty. During this first day, you will make sure that the child drinks lots of liquid. Eating salty snacks such as crackers can increase liquid consumption. This will ensure that the child is urinating often during the day, which means more potty time. Make a big deal out of it when your child uses the potty, creating a potty dance or a mini potty party to show your approval.

After the child goes in the potty about 12 times, he or she will begin going to the potty on their own. Of course, the child is going to have an accident and that is perfectly fine. Simply tell the child that it is okay, but explain that they are supposed to go in the potty. When you use this method, you are supposed to help the child clean up the mess they made, but it is important that you do not shame the child or get on to him or her for having an accident.

Before the child takes a nap or goes to bed at night, you will put training pants or a diaper on them unless you are sure that he or she will be able to stay dry while they are sleeping.

Eventually, you will feel safe venturing out of the house with your child. When this time comes, you will have the child wear baggy pants with nothing underneath, no diaper or underwear. This will make it easier for the child to use the potty when you are out.

It is said that by the end of the weekend, the child will be completely potty trained and that while they will have accidents just like other children, they will not need to go through the process of potty training again.

2. Time it right (You need a timer)

This is a method that many parents use when they first begin potty training. You will need a timer that makes a noise loud enough for both you and your child to hear and you will need to make sure that you are available when it is time for your child to potty.

You will also need a potty seat or little potty for your child to use. Each time that the timer goes off, you will take your child to the potty, have them sit on it and wait. You will wait until the child has used the potty, celebrate and reset the timer.

The timer will need to be set for about 20 minutes and you have to make sure that you do not miss any potty time. During this time, the child can wear potty training underwear or training diapers such as Pull Ups. You will let the child sleep in a diaper as well.

The pros of this technique are:

- The child does not feel pressured
- There are fewer accidents than with other methods
- The child is able to succeed quickly
- The child is able to pick up on potty training quicker
- Both you and the child will experience less frustration.

The cons of this technique are:

- Your child will be in diapers longer when this process is used
- You will have to continue to purchase training pants until the child is fully potty trained

If you don't mind purchasing diapers and training pants, this is a low stress technique that makes potty training easy on both the parent and the child.

3. Booty Camp

This process takes a bit longer and is usually used by parents that can be with the child full time while they are potty training. Some parents choose to take a week of vacation time in order to potty train using this technique, however it is much more successful for parents that stay at home.

This entire process will take about a month. You will begin by taking the child to the bathroom at regular intervals, when it is obvious that they need to go and after they have eaten a meal or had a drink. When you are using this process, you can choose to purchase Pull Up type training pants or you can continue to keep using diapers. It really does not matter which you choose, simply choose what works best for you.

During this process, you are going to talk to your child about using the potty, ask the child if they understand the sensations that happen when they need to use the potty and always ask the child if he or she needs to use the potty. This technique requires that you stay close to home in order to help the child get into the routine of using the potty instead of eliminating in his or her diaper however, it is a great technique to use when you are out and about as well.

If you do not mind, allowing your child to use public bathrooms or carrying a portable potty seat with you, all you have to do is remember to ask your child regularly if they need to use the potty. If there is an accident, it really is not that big of a deal because the child is still in a diaper. This of course means that unlike when you are using other methods, there will be nothing to clean up.

4. Reward Technique

I spoke a bit earlier in this book about using rewards in order to get your child to use the toilet instead of eliminating in their diaper.

You will show the child what their reward will be, explain to the child what behavior they need to display in order to get the reward and present the reward to the child after he or she uses the potty.

You can also have a larger prize for the child to work toward. For example, if you are using stickers as a reward, you can tell the child that if they collect a certain number of stickers that you will take them to grandma's house or to the store to purchase a small toy. Most of the time, this is the only motivation that a child needs when it comes to potty training. This also works for other behaviors.

The downside of this technique is that you may end up with a child that demands a reward every time they do something good and when they find out that is not going to happen, well, let's just say they have been known to show out a little bit.

In order to avoid this, you are going to have to know where to draw the line. Eventually, you are going to have to taper off on the rewards and start giving praise when your child uses the potty. This can be a difficult transition for both you and the child.

5. Easy Does It

This is another very simple way to potty train your child and it does not take a lot of time. You will begin by purchasing a potty seat and some training pants. Place the potty seat in the main room of your house and switch your child's diaper for training pants.

Explain to the child that instead of using the diaper to eliminate in, you want them to use the potty. Show them how to pull, the training pants up and down as well as how to sit on the potty.

Remind the child every 15-20 minutes that they are supposed to use the potty. You can also let the child walk around naked if you would like. One thing that I have learned is that children are interested in their new potty seats and will even sit on them while they are watching television.

Make it very clear that if the child is on the seat they are not to have a diaper on. Before you know it, they will go in the potty on their own and will be very proud of what they have done, often dragging you to the potty seat to show you their accomplishment.

Make a huge deal out of this. Dance, jump up and down, give them a high five and do whatever you can to make them feel as if they have accomplished something huge because after all, they have. If you make a big enough deal out of it, soon you will find that they have once again used the potty and you will know because they are proud enough to show you.

Continue making a huge deal out of it, for a few days. Then tone down on your reaction until it simply becomes normal for your child to use the potty.

Once your child has become accustomed to using the potty, move it into the bathroom making sure that you show the child where it is. By doing this, you will show the child that they are 'grown up' just like you.

This technique puts the child in charge. You are not dragging them to the bathroom, forcing them to sit with their feet on the cold floor, but instead they decide that they want to use the potty. Keeping the potty in the main room of the house is also going to make potty training easier. The reason for this is because one of the reasons that many children have accidents when they are potty training is because they don't want to miss out on what everyone else is doing. Keeping the potty in the main room is going to let the child know that they are not going to miss out on anything that might happen. It is also going to make them feel as if they are part of the group instead of separate, which is what can happen if you begin by placing the potty in the bathroom.

6. Spiderman Likes to Stay Dry

This is a great technique that you can use with children who have a favorite character. I spoke a bit about this technique a little earlier, but I want to go into more depth.

You will begin by going out and purchasing some underwear for the child that have their favorite character on them, you want to make sure it is someone that your child really loves.

When the child wakes up, take him or her to the bathroom, explaining that they are going to start using the potty that day, tell them that they even get a surprise.

After the child has used the potty, show them the new underwear focusing on which character is on them. Explain to the child that the character does not like to get wet and the character does not want to be pooed on. You can repeat this several times before placing the underwear on the child.

Now, instead of going through your day reminding your child to go to the potty, all you have to do is remind the child that the character on their new underwear does not want to get wet. You will be amazed at how often their little eyes light up as they run to the bathroom, **'rescuing' their favorite character from getting wet or dirty.**

7. Panty Time

This is the final technique that I am going to give you in this chapter and it is a very simple technique. When you choose to potty train your child, you will throw away all of the diapers (or at least put them away for when they are asleep), purchase some cute panties and have the child put them on. When you use this technique you need to be prepared for a few accidents, however, it is by these accidents that your child will learn. When the child wears panties, he or she is going to be able to feel the true wetness or mess that they have made in the panties, they are going to have to help clean themselves up and this will help teach your child that they should make it to the potty quicker next time they need to go.

Of course, these are not all of the techniques and you can use a mixture of the techniques or even come up with a technique of your own, as long as it works for you and your child.

Chapter 7-Special Needs Potty Training

Potty training a special needs child is going to be a bit more difficult. Of course, you need to understand that a special needs child is not going to be potty trained at the same age nor is it going to take the same amount of time as other children.

You do not want to push your special needs child when he or she is already facing enough difficulties, however, it is important to their future self-care as well as their self-esteem that you do help them learn how to use the potty.

This should be a celebrated time, not one that is dreaded. **<u>Your child is ready to potty train!</u>** You have to understand that your child is going to make mistakes, do not focus on these mistakes, instead, show your child that he or she is able to make progress if they just stick with it.

When you are potty training a child with special needs, you have to remember that it is not going to be a fast process.

There are a few different signs that you will have to watch for when you are preparing to potty train a special needs child.

Signs Your Special Needs Child Is Ready To Potty Train

- The child knows and can feel the difference between being wet and being dry.
- The child is keep a dry diaper for a minimum of two hours.
- The child knows when he or she needs to urinate or have a bowel movement.
- The child is able to dress or undress on their own or is ready to learn how to do so.

- The child is motivated to stop using diapers and start using the potty.

I spoke earlier in this book about how it took much longer to potty train my youngest son than it did my other two children. The reason for this was because he is a special needs child. Therefore, I did not even attempt to potty train him until after his third birthday and **it took several months for him to be completely potty trained.**

When it comes to potty training a special needs child, you need to not only make sure that the child is mentally prepared, but you also need to talk to the child's doctor before proceeding. The doctor is going to be able to examine the child and let you know how you will move forward as well as if you need any special equipment.

Of course, you need to prepare yourself for the challenges that lie ahead as well. Many special needs children do not even begin potty training until they are five years of age or older which means that they are much bigger than the two and three-year-old children that you may be used to potty training.

Size does matter when it comes to potty training your child not only because the little potties only come in one size, but because you will be having to lift the child, help the child undress and clean the child. This can put quite a strain on you and can be very stressful. If you have a child that likes to fight back, it could mean that you are going to end up in a few wrestling matches simply because you want the child to use the potty.

It is also very important that you talk to your doctor and

make sure that it is okay for you to begin potty training because there are many physical disabilities that can make it difficult for a child to potty train and there are even some that are going to make it completely impossible.

When you are potty training a child with special needs, you have to remember that it is not going to be a fast process. It can take up to one year to completely potty train a child with special needs, even if the disability is something like oppositional defiance disorder or ADHD.

Potty training a child with special needs presents its own set of challenges because depending on the type of disability that your child has, he or she could refuse to use the potty for a variety of different reasons. For example, the child may decide that they do not like the smell of the disinfectant used in the bathroom or even the feel of the tile on their feet. These are the types of challenges that a parent of a special needs child will face when they are potty training.

When you decide that it is time to begin potty training, you should begin paying attention to your child's elimination habits. Write down the times that your child has a wet or dirty diaper every day for about a week and look for a pattern. You may find that the child is actually eliminating at about the same time each day.

<u>After you have figured out what your child's pattern of elimination is, you will not get rid of the diapers and begin using training pants or panties</u>. Instead, you will take the child to the bathroom when you feel it is time for them to use the toilet, remove the diaper and place the child on the toilet.

Interact with the child as they are sitting, make sure that the child is relaxed because tight muscles are only going to make the potty training process harder. Sing a song, tell a story or look at a book together. With the technology that we have today, you can even allow the child to watch a few minutes of a video while they wait.

After the child has used the toilet, clean the child, explaining why you are cleaning him or her the way that you are and place a new diaper on the child. Take the child to the bathroom sink and have him or her wash their hands while you wash yours. After this is done, flush the toilet while the child is away from it so that you do not frighten the child.

When the child becomes comfortable with this process, you can allow the child to start wiping on their own, however, you need to make sure that the child is clean before putting a new diaper on the child. Eventually, you will find that the child is telling you when they need to use the bathroom and they are not eliminating in diapers any longer.

This is when you can purchase panties for the child to wear during the day, however, you should allow the child to wear a diaper when they sleep, especially if their disability stops them from getting out of bed in the middle of the night and using the bathroom on their own.

Potty training a child with special needs does take a bit more patience, but it is possible and you should never feel as if you are failing. **You have to remember that every child struggles when it comes to potty training, they have accidents and yours will as well.** Becoming upset or angry because your special needs child has had an accident is only going to cause your child to become upset and not want to try to use the potty.

No matter how long it takes to teach your child to use the toilet instead of eliminating in a diaper, stick with it. Do not give up because this is only going to confuse the child and make the process much harder in the future.

Chapter 8- How To Potty Training After Divorce or Separation

Potty training can be very difficult at times, when you are a single parent potty training it can seem even more difficult and when you have to deal with the other parent, either using a different technique or not potty training at all, it can seem completely pointless.

The first thing that you have to understand if you are potty training after a divorce is that you cannot potty train right after a divorce. This is a time when children usually regress and expecting them to learn a new skill may cause more stress than they can handle. You have to understand that going through a divorce is not only stressful for you, but it is stressful on the child as well.

Wait until life had gotten back to normal before you begin

potty training your child in order to ensure that they are able to meet the demands and focus on the task ahead of them.

If you had already begun potty training before the divorce occurred, you need to understand that the child is going to regress and you may see more accidents. This is not the time to get angry with your child or to take your aggression toward your ex out on your child. Instead, this is the time to show your child that you still love him or her, that you are not going anywhere and that it is not their fault that anything happened.

You are also going to have to be able to talk to your ex if you want to be able to continue potty training. It is very important that both of you are on the same page when it comes to potty training, the techniques that will be used and how potty training will be addressed in each house.

Both of you also have to understand that the child may have more accidents in the beginning because they are potty training in two separate houses. In order to cut back on the accidents, it is important that the setup is the same at each house.

If your child has a little potty at your house, he or she needs to have a little potty of their own at your ex's house. While these two do not have to be the same, it is best if they are because this is going to help the child feel more comfortable when using them. The familiar potty will almost be a comfort to them when they are using it.

If one parent has decided to use a potty seat over the regular toilet with a step stool, the other parent needs to have the same type of setup at their house. This will cut back on confusion and will set your child up for success.

<u>Both homes need to be set up the same way for potty training.</u> For example, if you are using a chart system as your reward system, both homes need to have the same chart as well as the same stickers so that the child earns the same reward at both homes.

This will provide consistency for your child and the familiarity will allow the child to feel safe and secure in both homes as well as when they are using the potty. **<u>The child's schedule must be kept exactly the same in both homes as well.</u>** This means that the child will eat at the same time in both homes, he will nap at the same time in both homes, he will sleep at the same time in both homes and he will use the bathroom at the same time in both homes.

<u>It is vital that diapers are not used at one home while being used at the other.</u> This can be very confusing for a child and it will make potty training take much longer than is necessary. If one parent is set on using diapers, put potty training off until a later date because the truth is, you are simply wasting your time and only frustrating your child.

When it comes to techniques and preparing your child for potty training, there is not much of a difference if the child is living in one home or in two. You will still need to ensure that your child is ready to potty train and make sure that no deadlines are set. **It is also vital to your child's success that both parents practice patience.** We have to remember that the child is just getting used to going back and forth between his or her parents, and on top of that, they are trying to learn how to use a potty which can be very stressful for them. Patience is key when it comes to potty training a child that has been through a divorce.

You also need to make sure that while you are potty training the child no other changes are made. For example, this is not the time to decide you want to sell your house. It is not the time to decide that you want to start dating and leaving your child with a new sitter nor is it the time to make any other big changes. There should only be one big change going on at this time and that is the transition that your child is going through, from diaper to potty.

It is understandable that there are some hurt feelings and you may not be communicating with your ex as much as you should. **If this is the case, if the two of you simply cannot sit down and be civil with each other, make a few notes and send them with your child when he or she goes to visit.** You should not create a book dictating how to raise the child when your ex has him or her but instead, jot down important points. Let your ex know what you are doing to potty train the child, send a copy of the training chart, stickers and a few pairs of training pants so that your child has everything that he or she needs while potty training. If you have to, you can even send their potty seat with them as long as you make sure your ex will return it with the child.

If all else fails, put potty training off until a later date. There are going to be times, circumstances when stopping is the best option. You should not look at it as giving up or failing, but simply pausing the process. Of course, this is never recommended because it can make potty training take longer in the future, however, if circumstances change so much while you are in the middle of potty training you have to decide if it is best to continue or if you should wait.

If you do choose to stop potty training, let your child know that it has nothing to do with them and that you will pick up potty training later. If you wonder if your child should be potty training or if they are under too much stress, there are a few signs that you can watch for.

Signs you should stop potty training.

- Your child is having a lot more accidents than before
- Your child looks stressed or tired all of the time
- Your child is cranky and does not want to potty train.
- Your child will not tell you when they need to go
- Your child is eliminating in unapproved areas, such as the closet.
- Your child is resisting using the potty even when you place him or her on it.
- Your child is holding urine or bowel movements.
- Your child is hiding when it is time to use the potty
- Your child is running way when it is time to use the potty

You are the only person that can determine if you should stop potty training for a short period of time and if you feel that it is causing more stress in your life than changing diapers would, there really is no reason to force the issue.

Remember, stopping potty training and putting it off until a later date does not mean that your child is never going to be potty trained. It simply means that your child is not going to be potty trained right now. It will happen in the future, no matter what.

If you do decide that you should stop potty training for a little while, listen to your child. There will come a point when your child is going to begin showing interest in the potty once again or they are going to start asking questions about when they can begin using the potty again. That is when you will know that they have calmed down and are no longer overly stressed because of the divorce or other changes that have happened in their life and they are ready to give it another go.

Conclusion-

It is my hope that while you read through this book that you began to understand that potty training does not have to be as complicated as many people would like to make it out to be. I hope that you have found a few tips and tricks that are going to help you potty train your child with ease and I hope that you have found a technique that will work for you.

Many preschools are taking in children that are as young as three years old, but one of the requirements is that the child must be potty trained. However, as you have learned in this book, potty training a child before their third birthday could make the process take much longer.

You should never feel that you have to potty train your child just because someone else says that it should be done, even if that someone else is their school. Remember, you can always put school off for another year, but you cannot undo the **damage** that is done by potty training too early.

While potty training is a very important skill that all children have to learn at some point or another in their lives, it does not have to be something that causes stress for the child or for the other members of the family. Instead, it is a time that should be celebrated. NO MORE DIAPERS! What should be celebrated more than that?

Finally, if you have worked through this book and have found that none of these techniques have worked for you, but you know that your child is ready to potty train, you should consider talking to a doctor.

****

If you want to learn more about how to change your life to positive thinking, this book will teach you everything from how to overcome negativity, how we sabotage our efforts toward positivity by talking negatively to ourselves, how stress and anxiety can affect our lives, and how staying healthy can help us be more positive, to the physical and mental tricks that you can employ to begin utilizing positive thinking in your life today.

Positive thinking can change us physically and emotionally, and they can provide us with a longer life and a plethora of physical health benefits. If this sounds or something that you would like to read more about, Changing Your Life Through Positive Thinking has the answers you need about how you can empower yourself and leave negativity behind you forever.

We can not raise a happy child if we are constantly screaming threats at them. No parent sets out to hurt their child, but this type of parenting does just that. To raise a happy child that wants to behave, you need to retrain yourself first. You need to change the way you think and react to their behavior.

You need to understand your triggers and heal yourself. Only then you can begin to heal your relationship with your children.

Did you enjoy reading this book? Can I ask you a favour?

Thanks for purchasing and reading this book, I really hope you find it helpful.

If you find this book helpful, **<u>please help others find this book by kindly leaving a review.</u>** I love getting feedback from my customers, loved it or hated it! Just Let me know. and I would really appreciate your thoughts.

Thanks in advance

Jennifer N. Smith

Check out my website below for more self-improvement tips and advice:

http://improve-yourself-today.com/

Did you enjoy reading
this book?

Please help others
find this book by
kindly leaving a
review.

Thanks in advance

Jennifer N. Smith

ABOUT THE AUTHOR

For me, the hardest part of being a mom is learning how to manage my own emotions. After having a baby, I found myself yelling at my husband and my son every day, I felt horrible and guilty afterward, and I felt so stressed and tired all the time.

I started reading lots of self-help books and I have learned a lot. Now, I feel happier and positive.

I want to share what I have learned throughout the years with my readers; I hope my books can help you deal with your day-to-day challenges, and make you feel happy again, you can create a home full of peace and love for the whole family.

Made in the USA
Middletown, DE
29 December 2018